Dogs

Julie Murray

Abdo
FAMILY PETS
Kids

abdopublishing.com

Published by Abdo Kids, a division of ABDO, PO Box 398166, Minneapolis, Minnesota 55439.
Copyright © 2016 by Abdo Consulting Group, Inc. International copyrights reserved in all countries.
No part of this book may be reproduced in any form without written permission from the publisher.

Printed in the United States of America, North Mankato, Minnesota.

052015

092015

 THIS BOOK CONTAINS
RECYCLED MATERIALS

Photo Credits: iStock, Shutterstock

Production Contributors: Teddy Borth, Jennie Forsberg, Grace Hansen

Design Contributors: Candice Keimig, Dorothy Toth

Library of Congress Control Number: 2014958423

Cataloging-in-Publication Data

Murray, Julie.

Dogs / Julie Murray.

p. cm. -- (Family pets)

ISBN 978-1-62970-900-0

Includes index.

1. Dogs--Juvenile literature. 2. Pets--Juvenile literature.   I. Title.

636.7--dc23

2014958423

Table of Contents

Dogs 4

Dog Supplies 22

Glossary 23

Index 24

Abdo Kids Code 24

Dogs

Dogs make great family pets.

Some dogs are big.

Some are small.

Some dogs have long hair.

Others have short hair.

8

Dogs need **exercise**.

Owen walks his dog.

Dogs like to run.

They like to play.

Dogs need food and water.

Emma feeds her dog.

Dogs need **grooming**.

This keeps them clean.

Dogs should see a **veterinarian**.

This keeps them healthy.

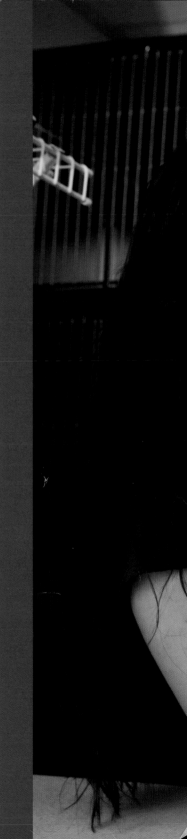

Is a dog the right pet for your family?

Dog Supplies

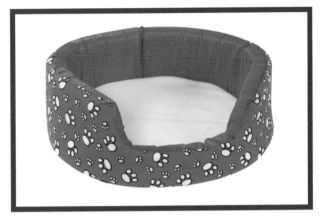

dog bed

dog leash

dog dish and food

dog toy

Glossary

exercise
a physical activity that makes
someone stronger and healthier.

groom
to take care of an animal's hair
by brushing or cleaning it.

veterinarian
a person who went to school
to treat hurt or sick animals.

Index

exercise 10, 12

family 4, 20

food 14

groom 16

hair 8

health 18

size 6

abdokids.com

Use this code to log on to abdokids.com and access crafts, games, videos, and more!

Abdo Kids Code:
FDK9000